MW01174146

Armadillo
and Friends

🦫 Dominie Press, Inc.

Señor Armadillo and his friends are going to town.

Señor Armadillo says
to Señor Coyote,
"You have good feet
for walking."

"Yes, yes," says Señor Coyote.
"I have good feet for walking."

Señor Armadillo says
to Señora Lizard,
"You have good feet
for climbing."

"Yes, yes," says Señora Lizard.
"I have good feet for climbing."

Señor Armadillo says
to Señor Jack Rabbit,
"You have good feet
for running."

"Yes, yes," says
Señor Jack Rabbit.
"I have good feet for running."

Señor Armadillo says
to Señora Chicken,
"You have good feet
for scratching
in the dirt."

"Yes, yes," says Señora Chicken.
"I have good feet
for scratching in the dirt."

Señor Armadillo says
to Señora Owl,
"You have good feet
for grabbing food."

"Yes, yes," says Señora Owl.
"I have good feet
for grabbing food."

"Stop! Stop!"
hisses Señora Snake.

Everyone stops.

Señora Snake says,
"If you want to talk about feet,
I will go home!"